D1146253

SEREN JAMES

the little book of
MOTIVATION

Hero, 51 Gower Street, London, WC1E 6HJ
hero@hero-press.com | www.hero-press.com

Contents © Seren James 2020
The right of the above author to be identified as the author of this work has
been asserted in accordance with the Copyright, Designs and Patents Act 1988.
British Library Cataloguing in Publication Data available.

Print ISBN 978-1-78955-1-198
Ebook ISBN 978-1-78955-1-204
Set in Times and Futura. Printing Managed by Jellyfish Solutions Ltd

Preface

We all need a little motivation in our lives. Whether it's a goal, something you aspire to in work, education or in your personal life.

The needs, desires or wanting to do something can escape us and we need to be stimulated in order to take action and achieve our goals. A little helping hand, positive and encouraging words is what this book is all about. Whether you use it for yourself or to offer advice to a friend, family, colleague, or teammate, there will be something for everyone. Even if it's just to make you smile.

Motivation

Whatever you are,
be a good one

ABRAHAM LINCOLN

The beginning is the most important part of the work

PLATO

If it is your passion,
you will succeed

Stop acting so small.
You are the universe in
ecstatic motion

RUMI

Willpower is the
biggest tool you
can have

Do the difficult things
while they are easy and
do the great things while
they are small. A journey
of a thousand miles must
begin with a single step

LAOZI

Be brave. Take
the leap

In the midst of chaos,
there is also opportunity

SUN TZU

There are no limits, only
you create boundaries

It doesn't matter how
slow you go as long
as you don't stop

CONFUCIUS

You are the
only limitation

The only person that can
push you, is you

We are all born
ignorant, but one
must work hard
to remain stupid

BENJAMIN FRANKLIN

If being successful
was easy – everyone
would do it

Expect the best – don't
expect to fail

Never, never never give up

WINSTON CHURCHILL

This is your moment

A somebody was a
nobody who wanted
to and did

JOHN BURROUGHS

All you need is a plan

You will never win if
you never begin

HELEN ROWLAND

Learn the rules of the
game and play better
than everyone else

Motivation comes from within

The secret of getting ahead is getting started

MARK TWAIN

The harder you work,
the greater the feeling
of achievement

To fail is to learn
how to succeed

Time is precious,
spend it wisely

Positive anything is better than negative nothing

ELBERT HUBBARD

The secret to success
is hard work and a
pinch of luck

Start by doing what is necessary, then what is possible, and suddenly you are doing the impossible...

ST. FRANCIS OF ASSISI

Success will happen,
however long it takes,
however many setbacks
you have

Re-evaluate and
understand the situation
– it will happen

Only those who have
the patience to do
simple things perfectly
will acquire the skill to
do difficult things easily

FRIEDRICH SCHILLER

Don't be afraid,
embrace change

Small opportunities are
often the beginning of
great enterprises

DEMOSTHENES

Fear is your greatest
obstacle

Well done is better than well said

BENJAMIN FRANKLIN

Goals are never easy
and when you score,
the feeling is incredible

Timing is everything

We can do anything,
but we can't do
everything

Vision without execution is just hallucination

HENRY FORD

Learn from other
people's failures
and don't repeat

There are no shortcuts
to success

Keep making the effort
and you will eventually
see results

Patience is a virtue

A person often meets his destiny on the road he took to avoid it

JEAN DE LA FONTAINE

If you are always trying to be good, you'll never be great

Some people look for a
beautiful place. Others
make a beautiful place

HAZRAT INAYAT KHAN

The noblest pleasure is the joy of understanding

LEONARDO DA VINCI

Don't run out of
ink. Inspiration is
everywhere

You can never cross the
ocean until you have
the courage to lose
sight of the shore

CHRISTOPHER COLUMBUS

Believe in yourself and
others will believe in you

If you fell down yesterday,
stand up today

H. G. WELLS

Look at what others
have done and
do better

Believe you can and you are halfway there

THEODORE ROOSEVELT

Take inspiration
and practices from
other successes

The beginning is
perhaps more difficult
than anything else, but
keep heart, it will turn
out all right

VINCENT VAN GOGH

Success is 75% appearance

LUCY CHAMBERLAIN

Happy people work better. Make sure to give yourself a break and enjoy life

P. J. SNICKLESON

Once you start working
on something, don't
be afraid of failure and
don't abandon it. People
who work sincerely are
the happiest

CHANAKYA

The most effective way to do it, is to do it

AMELIA EARHART

Don't think, just do

HORACE

The higher we soar, the
smaller we appear to
those who cannot fly

FRIEDRICH NIETZSCHE

The secret of getting ahead is getting started. The secret of getting started is breaking your complex overwhelming tasks into small manageable tasks, and starting on the first one

MARK TWAIN

Perseverance will
help achieve greater
professional success

Take a deep breath,
take a walk and clear
your mind – it will come

Take one step at a time

Knowing is not enough, we must apply. Willing is not enough, we must do

JOHANN WOLFGANG VON GOETHE

First say to yourself what
you would be; and then
do what you have to do

EPICTETUS

If you can't do it, find
someone else who can
and learn from them

Don't be an old bottle of shampoo. Do something

TED (AGE 4)

Reflect and look back
at what you have
achieved and know
that what is to come is
possible

If you need help – don't
fear rejection or shame

Just keep trying, you'll get there

ANNALIE (AGE 8)

If you don't ask you
don't get. If you don't
ask you'll never know

Set an end reward
for yourself or others
to complete a task,
project or objective

Our greatest weakness
lies in giving up. The
most certain way to
succeed is always to try
just one more time

THOMAS EDISON

Don't judge each day
by the harvest you reap
but by the seeds that
you plant

ROBERT LOUIS STEVENSON

Remind yourself of your goals. Make a list, however micro, and tick them off. By breaking it down, it will motivate you on your overall task

Be stronger than your
strongest excuse

Difficult roads often
lead to a beautiful
destination

A positive outlook and
character is contagious

A goal without a
plan is just a wish

Try and fail but don't fail to try

JOHN QUINCY ADAMS

Today is a new day
and a new beginning

Each day do your best
and let go of the rest

Focus all of your
energy, not on fighting
the old but on building
the new

SOCRATES

Make weekly
checkpoints to track
your progress

Feel it, see it,
hear it, make it

The mind is not a vessel
to be filled but a fire to
be kindled

PLUTARCH

There is something in
the human spirit that will
survive and prevail, there
is a tiny and brilliant light
burning in the heart of
man that will not go out
no matter how dark the
world becomes

LEO TOLSTOY

Make sure to reward
yourself every time
you achieve your
weekly goals

Watch and read
motivational stories
or speeches by those
you admire

Luck is what happens
when preparation
meets opportunity

SENECA

Have a vision for yourself. A vision should be large enough to keep you motivated...

If you follow your passion,
motivation will come

Read and listen to
inspiring stories that
will help you achieve
your goal

For success, attitude is
equally as important
as ability

WALTER SCOTT

You will always have good days and bad days. The bad days will help you get better as you won't want to make those mistakes again

Experiment with something new

Our greatest weakness
lies in not giving up.
The most certain way to
succeed is always to try
just one more time

THOMAS EDISON

Find a partner, friend or colleague to bounce ideas and to help bring you back on track

Reward yourself on the accomplishment of a goal or objective. A treat or some other "indulgence" can go a long way in keeping you motivated

Your limitation – it's only
your imagination

Sometimes later
becomes never, so do
it now and get over the
hurdle

Nothing can stop
the man with the right
mental attitude from
achieving his goal

THOMAS JEFFERSON

Change your view
or perspective,
sometimes hanging
upside down can give
you the answers

Negative thoughts is
the single greatest
obstacle to success

Nothing is particularly
hard if you divide it
into small jobs

HENRY FORD

He who is not
courageous enough to
take risks will accomplish
nothing in life

Action is needed
because knowing
is not enough

Stop thinking and
just do it. If you get
it wrong start again

Quality is not an act – it is a habit

ARISTOTLE

Having ambition is
the path to success

Believing it can be
done is half the battle

Have clarity and a
clear mind to focus
on what lies ahead

A challenge may not
always be fun but
you'll feel great once
you've achieved it

You must have
confidence in your
competence

Good thoughts make
happy days

Forget the risk
and take the fall,
if it's meant to be,
then it's worth it all

ANON

A little more persistence,
a little more effort, and
what seemed hopeless
failure may turn to
glorious success

ELBERT HUBBARD

It is never too late to be what you might have been

GEORGE ELIOT